THESAURUS
OF
SEPARATION

THESAURUS OF SEPARATION

TIM MAYO

ISBN 978-1-927496-10-7

Cover artwork by Amelia X.
Design, calligraphy and editing by Elizabeth Adams

First Edition
©2016 Tim Mayo

Published by Phoenicia Publishing, Montreal
www.phoeniciapublishing.com

For Amelia X.
November 1, 1961–March 10, 2013

Acknowledgments

Grateful thanks to April Ossmann who edited the very first and incomplete version of this manuscript, to Patricia Fargnoli, good friend, confidant and fellow poet, to Meg Kearney, Jeff Freidman, Elizabeth Ungerleider, and also to my deceased partner, Amelia Hancock, who preferred the anonymity of "Amelia X.," whose artwork graces the cover of this book, and to whom this book is dedicated, and who so supportively witnessed the making of so many of these poems during our five years together. Also deserving thanks for their help and long-time support are my friends and poets, Charles S. Rogers, Martha Ramsey, Verandah Porche and Tom Ragle, and finally, to my loving partner, Andrea Livermore, who has stood by me with the patience of Job and given me advice and support in the long process of arranging, rearranging and rewriting these poems ad infinitum so as to finally arrive at this place, this book.

Lastly, a grateful thanks to the following publications and their editors for publishing the following poems in this collection:

Journals

Anthem Journal: "How the Old Make Love . . ."

Avatar Review: an earlier version of "Foster Home" entitled "All You Can Tell" and an earlier version of "Boarding School" entitled "The Closeness"

Barrow Street: "Squirrel Song"

Blue Lake Review: "After Reading the Master, I Stay Inside" and "Hiroshige: Near Komakata"

Chrysalis Reader: an earlier version of "Stone" ("Time, Bomb")

Connotation Press: An Online Artifact: "Puppet Therapy," an earlier version of "Trapezing in God's Country" and an earlier version of "Working in Detox"

Crab Creek Review: an earlier version of "Possibilities for a Final Love Poem"

Driftwood Press: "Chasing the Bear from the Birdfeeder"

5AM: "Five-Story Walk-Up"

Kentucky Review: "The Woodbine's Song"

Narrative Magazine, poem of the week: "The River Merchant's Answer to his Wife"

Naugatuck River Review: "Independence Day," "Meat" and an earlier version of "Portrait of the Real Toad"

New Millenium: "Bowing to the Miniscule" (Honorable Mention in their 39th Poetry Contest)

OVS Magazine: "Learning the Letter O," "The Yellow Afternoon," "My Daughter Sings her Daily *Bhajan*"

Poet Lore: "Constant Replay," "The Trucker's Tale" and "The Only Picture"

Rat's Ass Review: "Crow" and *"La Belle Dame Sans Merci"*

Redheaded Stepchild: an earlier version of "As if in Heaven," "Talking to the Dead" and "Leaving Brahms, an Elegy"

Redux: A Literary Journal: for reprinting online "The Remedy"

River Styx: "The Remedy"

Salamander: "Every Poet Needs a Brother"

San Pedro River Review: "Self-Storage"

Tar River Poetry: "Taxonomies"

Truck (an online literary magazine & blog): "Playing with Szymborska"

Valparaiso Poetry Review: "Shelter"

Verse Wisconsin: "The Uncapping"

Anthologies

The 100 Thousand Poets for Change Anthology, 2011: "Constant Replay" and "Five-Story Walk-Up"

Birchsong: Poetry Centered in Vermont: "The Uncapping"

Best Indie Lit New England Anthology for 2012: "Learning the Letter O," "Independence Day"

Contents

Acknowledgments vi

Mourning Among Strangers 5

Little Reverie at the Keyboard 9
Yellow Afternoon 11
Learning the Letter *O* 13
Taxonomies 15
Words 17
Playing with Szymborska 19

Possibilities for a Final Love Poem 23

Darning Eggs 27
The Only Picture 28
Foster Home 31
Talking to the Dead 32
The Trucker's Tale 35
Squirrel Song 36
Thin 39
Bowing to the Miniscule 41

Self-Storage 45

Mail Man 49
Crow 51
Meat 52
The Remedy 55
Boarding School 58
My Daughter Sings Her Daily *Bhajan* 61
After Reading the Master, I Stay Inside 62

Shelter 67

La Belle Dame Sans Merci 71
Stone 72
Puppet Therapy.. 74
Independence Day 77
Working in Detox... 78
Five-Story Walk-Up 81
Trapezing in God's Country 82
As if in Heaven 86
Leaving Brahms, an Elegy 88
Wish you were here in Sober City 90

Hiroshige: Near Komakata... 95

Constant Replay 98
Coffee To Go 100
Chasing the Bear From the Birdfeeder 103
The Woodbine's Song... 105
Every Poet Needs a Brother.. 106
Portrait of the Real Toad 109
The River Merchant's Answer to his Wife.. 111
Gran'mère Shows Us Her Crooked Finger 113
How the Old Make Love 114

The Uncapping 119

Notes.. 122
About the Author... 125

The Body grows without—
The more convenient way—
That if the Spirit—like to hide
Its Temple stands, alway,

Ajar—secure—inviting—
It never did betray
The Soul that asked its shelter
In solemn honesty

Emily Dickinson

How happy is the little Stone
That rambles in the Road alone,
And doesn't care about Careers
And Exigencies never fears—
Whose Coat of elemental Brown
A passing Universe put on,
And independent as the Sun
Associates or glows alone,
Fulfilling absolute Decree
In casual simplicity—

Emily Dickinson

Mourning Among Strangers

To some extent, they were all strangers
to *him*, as they gathered around her bed,
impatient for death to assuage what they
imagined was her suffering. He was their
father, freed at the last minute from his wife,
the fairy tale's standard step-mother,
to breech the continental divide and say
goodbye to a daughter he hadn't seen
or spoken to in twenty-odd years . . . and,

though guilty of the same transgression,
certainly *I*—the interloping lover, professed kin
to no one—*I* was a stranger to them all:
the father sitting opposite the tightly knit
sisters and brothers, their husbands and wives,
all of whom had found it so understandably
difficult to live with her plight, thus always
wondering how I could possibly . . . so,

it was there, in those last, long hours,
gnawing on the cheese and crackers of guilt
and grief given to us by those kind attendants
at the old folk's home, who housed her
for her last few days—though she was young
by their standards—it was there,
as I read out loud some innocuous poem
I can't remember, now—mine
or someone else's—which had
seemed so appropriate at the time
but wasn't to her father . . . yes,

it was definitely there
that I learned how easy it was,
among strangers, to let one's grief
get in the way of another's.

Little Reverie at the Keyboard

All night, the wind gusts, huffing
like a bear; spits of rain
luff on the roof, diminish

into unpredictable patter, then
lessen, even more, in the hushed air
like remnants of a sermon I nod off to.

What do they mark,
those little syllables of splash?

Is their language that different
from the wren?

And isn't warble just a dialect of Big Beard:
the old man we like to robe in clouds,

then thrust a lightning bolt into his hand
and call him reverent names?

I know him. He talks down to me
all the time.

Not because power plays into him,
it's just where we've placed him
in the grand scheme of things:

hung him so high
on the cosmological yardarm
it hurts our necks.

So, maybe, I'll invite him down
to the poop deck, face to face,
to talk turkey and thunderbolts . . .

The wind rises again. Rain
spatters down fat leaves,
ta-tums on the tin roof.

Yellow Afternoon

How many more times will you remember a certain afternoon of your childhood, some afternoon that's so deeply a part of your being that you can't even conceive of your life without it? Perhaps four or five times more. Perhaps not even that. . . .
Paul Bowles

Once, you woke and saw the afternoon
tinted yellow as if a lens had walled
you from it; a jaundiced pall
had spread across the cirrus sky
and made the green lawn seem greener.

Kids you didn't know mimicked tops.
Laughing, they spun their bodies,
arms outstretched, canting their hands,
whirling faster and faster until house
blurred into hedge—tree—lawn, until
giddy from spinning, they tumbled
down to watch the sky rearrange itself,
then stop to hover above like a silent parent.

You wanted to join their play, you wanted
the yellow to go away—you wanted . . .
what we all want: the inexplicable to be
explained, and the egg shell of answers
to close over the yolk of our questions.

Learning the Letter *O*

You enter school at the letter *O*, having no idea
about the *A, B, C*'s of otherly significance.
Already, the teacher is talking them through it,
leaning over each child's shoulder, her lips

brushing their hair, her hand guiding their uncertain
little wrists through each round and shaky sweep
they try to make, whose success you only suppose.

And you, too, try to trace this bosomy curve, to wrap it
around a mothered sense you need to round out,
then return your unschooled hand to your beginning
with a penman's sureness, but your circle cannot hold.

So you flee into the unencumbered autumn, unable
to write that one, fundamental letter all lovers cry out
at least once in the unfolding literacy of their lives.

Taxonomies

In the Bible, one of them names the animals,
and to tell you the truth, I'd always assumed
that Adam really had. That's the first mistake
about being on top, you just assume the position.

So when a woman I knew, a poet, published how
Eve was the one slipping under the apple boughs,
turning over the leaves of grass, walking out,
pen in hand, into the open fields, to scribble

down the names each would carry for the rest
of Man's specious reign on Earth, I suddenly knew
that was how myth changes: first, a deep
annunciating thump arrives in your ribcage,

then, you twist the smooth pages of the old story,
crumpling them up and flattening them out, scratching
their surface until the ink relinquishes its authority,
and the words tell it the way you've always felt

it should be.

Words

When the first person I saw said one, I knew
none, as I gesticulated with my chubby legs
and arms, with my lips and toothless gums.

Since then, words have come to me like barrels
rolling over the waterfall of my tongue:
each with its own crazed body within

seeking the sensations of its own existence,
and I have fallen for them spilling them back
into an undigested world.

But is that how we know? We touch our mouths,
then throw out the hungered content as if blowing a kiss
to where meaning falls seeking its own level?

—Or do we intuit:

smacking our lips with a new wisdom from within,
the electric *savoir faire* spitting out of the brain
its pop and spark toward epiphany?

I once had an imaginary friend. He had invisible hair,
a see-through smile, and was always silent,
withholding judgment. We parted ways,

and a subtle knowledge settled in
as when the lonely put away childish things
and enter the fellowship of the grown.

There were no words for him, no stone,
no teething of noise with all its
attendant gnashing and attitudes.

Playing with Szymborska

In the lost paradise of improbabilities,
we arrive at our sand box.
We dig our toes into the clean
but gritty inches of its landscape
ready to make the best of everything.

Although I have brought to this place
the inappropriate noises of my little red truck,
the sound of its spinning wheels in the sand,
I marvel at the subtle castles she builds,
the whimsical, rising twirls to her modest towers.

I want to know her gift for suspension, how
when her little figures fall from their twin towers,
marking the air like desperate ants,
they never land. I want to find the little keys
and coins I see dropping from their pockets
to become the archeology of their lives.

I want to dig their shards out of the sand,
piece them into poems fanning their pages
into wings which will also never land.

I want to do this with Szymborska,
her hand showing my fist how
to knock at the stone's door.

Possibilities for a Final Love Poem

Because you want emotional complexity
and a set of matching metaphors to go with it

which will convey all the nuances you need
for this poem to gather its hooves like a hunter
and take the passionate bent knees of your words

over the hurdles of expression, galloping
on into the homestretch to then relax

into that quivering but satisfying gait
you will need for your final couplet,

because you want all of this—both
the puissance and the subtlety—you must
scurry into the nether regions of your brain,

plugging every neuron into its neighbor,
searching through the electric bric-a-brac
of incompatible things which fill your skull:

a shoebox full of brown-edged letters
in a language you no longer speak,
the pages crackling with their fragile age,

an old saber from your cavalier days
with a light rust spreading like measles
across its blade,

               or lastly, this tarnished
trophy of a swimmer: poised to leap,
her once-silver gracefulness now leaning
her long, marbled body's discolorations
over the lip of a hollow urn—

this is the woman whose memory
ripples through you like a stone.

Darning Eggs

I remember their perched shapes: each tadpoled
to a spindle at its bottom which you held
as you slipped your sock over the bulbous end
to then begin the parsimony of your repair.
I'd never seen such polish:

the swirling, rich-brown, Circassian burl
you felt you could almost enter, a mysterious
burnt umber of clouds captured in an oval
almost nippled at the end, an entry to a kind of
mending I was too young to learn.

In a set of internet directions, someone
suggests an incandescent bulb, which, also,
is going the way of the darning egg,
as I search the hardware store finding only
the pigtail, fluorescent worms of today.

Now in my memory's underlit museum, the low
glow of the dimly-remembered intensifies, and I
see my foster sister sitting beside me: her dangling
legs pumping like mad pendulums, as her fingers
begin to mend what even time will never heal.

The Only Picture

Looking at the only picture of my father and me,
a creased-shut, black-and-white view
unfolding into cloudy shades of gray,

I am struck by our physical likeness,
that is to say, not how we look in the picture,
where I am young and pudgy beyond despair,

but how I see myself, now,
in his face and lean body leaning down
to hold my up-reached hand.

I say to myself, I have that same kindness
toward strangers as he must have had
toward me when he came to visit.

But I don't remember the visit, and so,
I don't remember if there were others,
and what I might have shown him
of the little world I lived in:

how in the backyard the grass
sloped green down to the watery lip
of a brown and brackish pond,

how it was a bitter mixture
of water to the tongue, how a similar
water, salty with the lives of little things

we cannot see, also runs through our blood
making the most of our bodies, how when
you take this universe away, all that's left

is a small residue of flesh and bones
we can never seem to shake from ourselves,
and what you don't know about this story

beyond the existence of this photo
and all its inherent suppositions
is—my sole epistemology.

Foster Home

All you can tell is that someone
must have said, *Smile*, and you did,

squinting out into the gray air
as if it were bright, but your father

presses his lips together, seeming
to brace for something you couldn't see.

Behind you, a lone hortensia
 completes the picture

as though putting her arms
around you both.

It has no blossoms. The full flourish
of its leaves hides

the complicated twists
of its branches.

And neglect has put this crease
you see through your father's heart,

so, now, it folds
and closes like a card.

Talking to the Dead

Late at night, you come
back like a police car,
black and white, prowling
the shadowed streets,
looking for the house
you left, the burglar
trying to get back in.

My suicide never came.
Back and forth in my head,
it roams like an ambulance
lost in the streets.
I still hear it wailing
toward hospital or home.
I'm never sure.

But for you, my dear,
dull from the lead
of one bullet
ripping your top off
like a rocket, you left
through a hole
in the side of your head.

Oh, which home
do I live in?
the one you killed—
or the one I've made?
Now, at odd hours,
a mailman knocks
at the door.

He adds this address
to a list on his fingers.
Who am I? he asks.
Your sister's keeper,
my uncle, the one I forgot,
who canceled himself
in the Post Office parking lot.

The Trucker's Tale

My son is three. He looks at me as if
yesterday's doors were always open.

He takes me by the hand
and leads me to his favorite toy:
a tin saucepan's battered lid
he steers around the yard
shifting it at the hip.

Tractor-trailer, car, or truck—
you can't tell which.
Then in a tongue I think I know,
he invites me to his secret place,
where the water falls from the mill run
and the sycamores line the shore.

I climb onto the bed of his wagon,
the one in which he's hauled the bulk
of all his little yearnings down
the brief commerce of his life.

He leads me to a flowering tree.
We climb up into its blossoms,
into the cradle of its crown,
where we stretch along the one,
low limb that leans out
above the mill pond's stilled surface,

and there, we watch the minnows flash
like fingers looking for a hand.

Squirrel Song

Washington, D.C.

The winter I was adopted, I, too, adopted
a small gray fellow who learned to come begging
at the kitchen's closed back window.

We lived in the capital of plenty,
in a dated lingo somewhere between *hobo*
and *homeless*. Frigidaires rose monolithic

and white from the low place I stood.
Their chrome trim was modest, and marble
lavished the grand façades of government,

but squirrels still foraged high and low
among winter's flagging leaves.
Boys still had freckles and Keds,

girls wore pigtails with colored bows,
patent leather shoes, and backdoors
were meant for other people.

Each day I fed my squirrel before school,
even before my Cream of Wheat
with its little butter pat melting in the middle

like a square sun. Then after winter
peeled off its white adhesive, revealing
the welting brownish black earth beneath,

after feeding the squirrel peanuts,
I went out into the backyard
to play alone in the dirt.

I witnessed armies of black ants
gird their loins and go forth.
I even intervened

aiding their march with a stick.
Time passed, boredom
fell upon me like a thief.

I looked about the yard. The ants
had long retreated into their holes,
the squirrel had gone its squirrelly way,

untouched by my nutty benevolence,
and the backdoor was closed
against the invisible cold.

Only my sharpened stick
pierced the earth.

Thin

Who could have ever known
that inside this skinny frame
there once lurked a fat man
tipping the scales operatically?

How the balloon of my being
blew up to a point
no body could hold?

Memories—untold memories—
held singular sway
over a vast concentration

of brain to body

to attempt to balance
my ever bloating self.

What does one remember
that cannot be uttered?

That makes the bottle
mute with cork?

That gathers in
all that can be gathered
like a winter's store
for a season's discontent?

A lifetime, yes, a lifetime,
squirrelled itself
deep down in layers
of fleshy softness,

then unpeeled,
cured like a prune,
to reveal its stone.

Bowing to the Miniscule

Each day you bow to the family
of fruit flies flitting about
the banana peels of your garbage.

You turn to the mosquito and bless it
with a gentle wave of your hand,
praying it to live without blood.

But it's not enough that you bow to
and bless the miniscule animals
of the world, their oozing larvae.

You must learn to go beyond, to kiss
the cold stone of the mountain, to press
your lips against the invisible beings

of the air, to abide they are there,
yet never swallow their poison,
and you must accept the perennial fly,

its karmic place in your ointment.

Self-Storage

It's not really the self that's in there—
more like all the forgotten parts of your life
you intended to revisit:

the swimming trophy you crawled miles to win
or the gold stars on a third grade calendar
marking the few days
of the one week in your life you behaved.

Then there's those pants
you think you'll sweat yourself back into.

They lie folded among the paste trinkets of time,
the jewels of your memory.

But what if you could . . .
just cinch up the whole girth of your life,
then flatten your beliefs
right out of your gut

(ironing out those wrinkles you keep stumbling over)

and fold your whole kit and caboodle of a body
(brain included with all its loose connections)

into some old snakeskin suitcase lying around
with its rusty lock and faulty hinges, then wait

the long humble moment it takes
to, at last, be carried away?

Mail Man

He lists up the walk lugging his heavy bag
full of the missives of bills and business:
ads for the carwash, a white sale or the splendid
array of utensils at the local hardware—all of this

weighs into his body as you begin to imagine
Hugo's hunchback whose lumpy animal yearnings
swelled to operatic proportions as he looked down
at the dancing girl from the high, ding-dong place

where love & lust break out like bells deafening
all those who desire the grand arias yet settle
for the small click-clack of little white letters
dropping into their brassy slots day after day.

Crow

I've been thinking how this poem
comes and goes as the crow flies,

picking at the raw red pieces of me
it finds smeared between the yellow lines
of my road—how a poem can hover

over the flesh and sinews of the spirit
so all you feel of the sky

is a piercing needle of want
as the poem's long beak
pokes at all your wanting parts.

So what I have wanted—no—needed—
is for this poem to open

its dark metaphoric wings, to take flight
with that one last piece of me
in its beak, to carry it to your nest,

weave the long skinny sinew of it
into the delicate mesh of your twig-lined house,

to let it nestle in your soft egg-haven,
and then to make you have of me

more than this small spurt of poetry
this bird insinuates into your life.

Meat

Like a spotted cat in a cage,
she slinked back and forth
on one of those sleek graphite slabs
with a rolling cylinder beneath—and I,

I exerted myself across the room
on one of those other, inexplicable devices
with a dull patina, where you sit straight up,
open your arms and present yourself

as a perfect specimen
of a spread-eagled bug.

That's when she looked at me
just as I pressed my arms together,
flexing into a pose only a machine
or vanity could put you in,

where your upper body bunches over
to cover your heart, your biceps
bulge against the big machine,

and your back muscles,
spreading out around your ribs,
start to hood like a cobra.

I recognized her look: a hunger
she didn't even know she had
dropped into her eyes,

then slid on as quickly as it came.

Men do this all the time;
they see a woman: her hair,
a slight curve of thigh,
or something else about her
triggers it,

and a part of them suddenly unfetters
into a falcon released from its master.

Out of view, it starts to circle for that mental place
to swoop and dive, lunge and tear off
a special piece of her,

some tender and erogenous part
where the body meets the psyche,

and the prey never even has a prayer.

The Remedy

You were fat in those days: neglect

had slipped like a towel from your waist
showing the whole world the soft rolls of yourself.

How it all glowed under your skin
like a radium dial,

becoming in the end:
a thick envelope for a thin heart.

And on summer nights, when the heat
dripped off the leaves like fat caterpillars,

you'd hang out sniffing cognac, putting on airs
in the only class restaurant around.

Those were the days when *haute cuisine*
were still foreign words
meaning something more than meatloaf.

How it moved you purposely along
up an invisible ladder
toward some new decorum.

Still, you dared to ask the slim dishwasher,
her first night ever on a job,

to go for a swim after work.

She was a young slip of a blonde with corkscrew hair,
whose father had wired your house and whose lightning wrath
you had never known,

but always feared
like a biblical child fears his Maker.

Nonetheless, somewhere in that part of your brain,
where things dwelled under the surface,
as quiet as crocodiles,

you both knew the pitter-patter
and thump of your intent.

*

There is a safety in numbers
when a handful of strangers all disrobe together
in the sweltering privacy of their own dark space.

Everyone concentrates so hard
to liberate their right foot
from the left leg of their lonely lives,

they see nothing else, and nakedness goes unnoticed.

The two of you slip into the water
as pat as opposable thumbs.

You swim out to the raft
where a host of faceless bodies
loll about like Romans.

The idea of numbers is still in play.

Then, one by one, the faceless bathers
roll off the raft and swim away,

taking with them the peeled grapes
and nibbling minnows of their hands,

and only the two of you are left to count the stars.

*

You know how it is about the dark,

how even in a moonless sky
the night stars can seem strong enough
to show you things as if it were day.

That's when you noticed
the statuary-beauty of her body,

(as if your art had suddenly found art)

but what you remember most about that night,

as you stood watching

her leggy presence
cross and uncross itself,

before she reached up to, finally,
clasp her hands behind the bustle of curls
bedding her head

—so unabashedly at ease—so unafraid—willing to show you—

every delicate portion and pocket
of her being,

is that it was hard to believe she was *that young,*
and that you did not touch her—not out of fear—
nor youth—nor even any unwritten law of decency—

but out of an inkling that, one day, this memory
of her fearless poise would be more precious
to you than what you sought.

Boarding School

I remember a roommate who never undressed
in my presence.

I never gave it a thought, till one day
I saw his bare white backside,

its hairless porcelain-patina,
before he turned as I entered

unexpectedly. He fled as a shy animal
on the verge of extinction might slip

through the leaves, so when you see it,
you think you've only imagined it.

What I'm trying to say
is my roommate had a tail.

A small wagging stub of a thing
at the end of his spine

just above the split in his buttocks
before they curved under giving
a slightly more simian slump

to his posture than the rest of us
who walked through the world.

Though I've kept silent about this for years,
I feel this need—not to shout it to the world

or poke you in the ribs as if it were
some freaky locker room joke.

Instead, as I have come to an age
I thought distant then,

I know now how close
we all are to our origins,

and as I look out my window
at the snow white, slouching
bows of the season,

I think I see a shape
slip deeper into the trees,

something unspeakably
hairless and pure

ghosting above the white ground.

My Daughter Sings Her Daily *Bhajan*

In the predawn of dreams before the sun wilts
the indigo flower of night, my daughter rises
from her bed, leaves all thoughts of flesh behind,
to walk barefoot over carpets of plush resplendence

into the still-silent ashram. There, she waits
for the sitars to find their place up and down a scale
that strums strange to my ear and for a tabla
to tap quietly at the door of her faith.

                                        Then
amid the drone and pluck of instruments, from deep
in her diaphragm, vowels rise up to the consonance
of an ancient tongue no longer sung except in prayer.

How does it feel to voice a language reserved only
for devotion, to be able to brush away in a gentle gesture,
as you sing, all the great vexations swarming about you?

After Reading the Master, I Stay Inside

If the divine has lost its capital D,
                              who cares?
                                              There is something else
about belief
             that goes beyond it,
                             coins a new word still to be sung
signifying warmth—not fire—
                        all the soul needs, a quiet passion
comfort does not consume.

The page I type this poem on has no substance.
                                     It hangs
like a square moon I click up
                    onto a blue screen.
So when an invisible turbulence
                           blows through the trees outside,
sending the green fetters of their limbs
                             flurrying through the real,
will this screen shake?
                  My vision of poetry blur?
                                    Will
this moon tumble down,
               turn trapezoid—its angles no longer
right?

      I dream of Chinese lanterns I will never see,
                                       their red
opaque glow signifying ancient mysteries,
                           each paper form
veiling its precarious fire,
                     and beneath them all,
                                   a shadow mimes a song.
Its dark, drunken arms gesticulate
                       all the melodious vowels to words
I have yet to make.

I purse my lips into a silver coin's shape,

but they emit neither song nor whistle.
There is no Empress to keep awake.

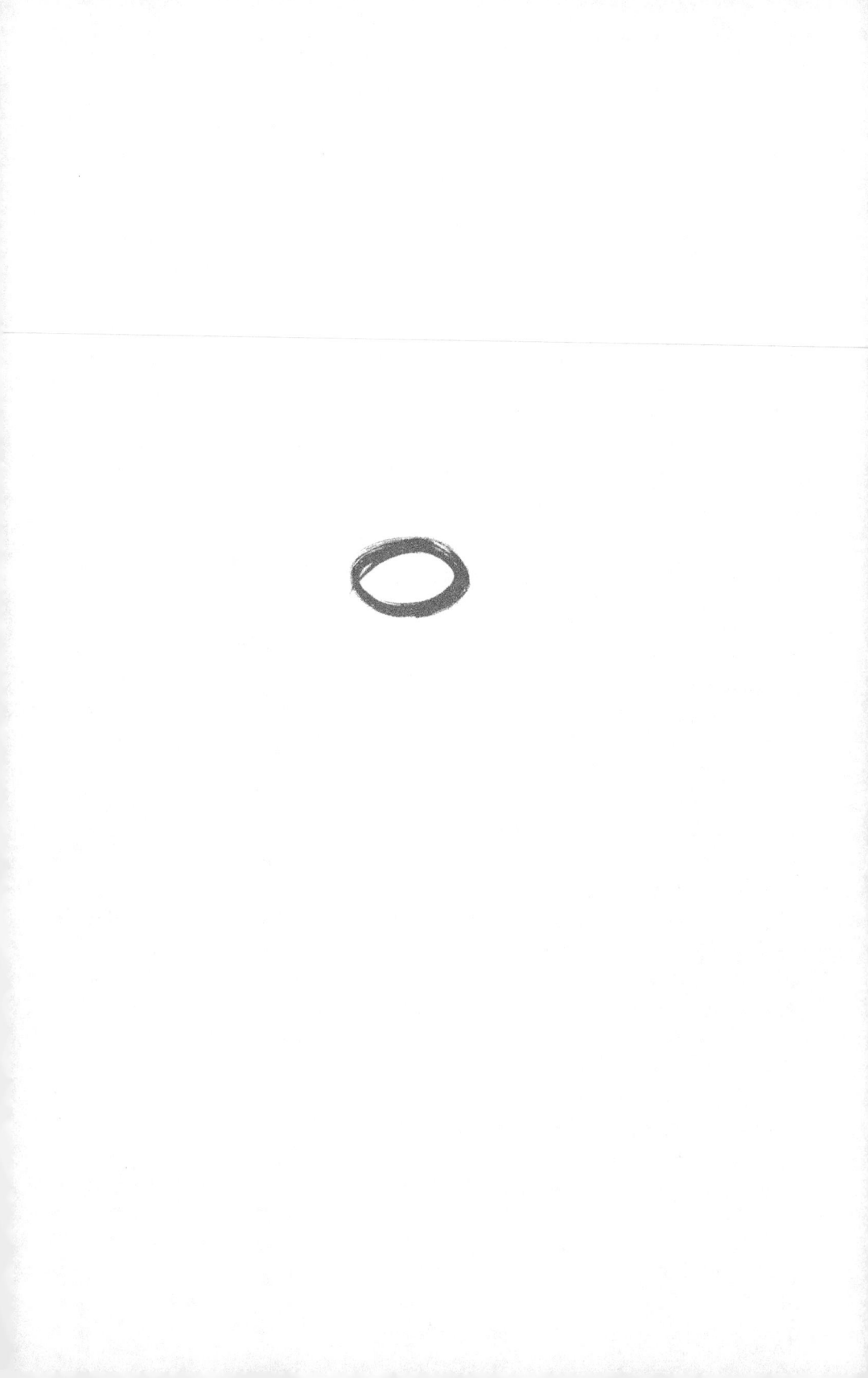

Shelter

> *Whenas in silks my Julia goes . . .*

When with her step, slide-step, my Amelia finally went,
no one, bedside, even thought about her clothes:

those pilled, goodwill hand-me-downs she used
to wear, which didn't flow—nor even scintillate.

I thought about the soul's betraying shelter:
her lame side limping, goose-fleshed & numb,

as her silent chugging intent lugged her spirit,
its brave vibration, over cobble and curb,

body propped by a cane & the crutching weight
of a silver-colored brace which bent her leg back

hyperextending the slow lope of her gait
into an unwilling liquefaction of limb.

Others saw some shaded piece of air
rise like a smoke ring: perfectly formed.

La Belle Dame Sans Merci

Then my dinner partner, a long gloved beauty,
up to her elbows in satin, a beauty of a certain age,
whose silver hair fell in casual perfection
over the delicate bones of her shoulders,

turned to me, tilting her long-stemmed glass,
ever so slightly, and fluttering her languorous lashes,
interjected herself into my most private of thoughts,

*Death is the ultimate spiritual act,
and for such fulfillment, such sublimity,*
mon petit bonhomme, *it must happen* au lit . . .
a queen-size at the very least, n'est-ce pas?

She waited, not for my reaction, but for my answer,
my clever parry to her conversational thrust,
for hers was a ploy to engage me in that verbal duel
and favorite pastime the French are so fond of.

The subject is never important, but the grace
and manner with which one addresses it are utmost:
the richness of innuendo and wit, the subtle deftness
of all the possible linguistic twists and turns,

and any reference to the personal is considered
an indiscretion of gross proportion.

I was speechless,

which had also been my previous state as I
pondered how her gown's neckline scooped away
from her collarbone, allowing me to gaze upon
her small, but still perfect, pear-shaped breasts.

I wondered if the rosettes of her nipples
had ever suckled a child. Somehow, they seemed
virginal to me, then, I wondered about death . . .
weren't we all virgins to its seduction?

Stone

That summer, Whitney is my bunkmate.
We play marbles all the time.
It's about all he can do.

Everyone says he's got rocks in his head—
lost his marbles—that his brain's between
a rock and a hard place we can't imagine.

We bunk in the cabin nearest the latrine,
where the counselors prep to blast
the big boulder high as my nine year old hip.

It's stood there since the ice age,
and we've always made our path
around it each time we go to pee.

For weeks before the big event, we watch them
pounding on a heavy steel rod to chip and tease
a hole deeper and deeper into the stone, letting
the salt air wash white into the brain-colored wound.

With each strike the big steel rings and digs
a little further. The hole it gouges
must go at least a foot—deep enough
for one stick of dynamite
to blow the rock's heart so far apart
only the eye-stinging dust of its memory
will remain.

So every day, after breakfast, the camp air
fills with the arrhythmic toll of the sledge
hammering against the rod: the sound
a constant, out of step, ding and stutter,
a little like a town clock gone awry,
its erratic, clunking chimes echoing
through the trees, keeping a different time
than the one we live by.

Here, the bugle blows the only hours we need to know.
We rise to Reveille, Assembly sounds, we sleep at Taps,
and twice a day a little toy cannon, so real our hearts stop,
puffs and booms our bright flag up and down a pole
to the bugle's tune—its pomp so noble
we all snap to attention! We all salute! . . .
indivisible and with justice for all.

Finally the moment comes, at the quiet hour
just after lunch, when no bugle blows and we go
to nap in our cabins, but today, we're admonished
to keep away from the windows.

They have no glass, these windows.
They are just squares of air: each with its own
wooden flap that hinges down at summer's end
only to close the cabin for winter,
only to keep all the unwanted critters out,
but no one thinks to close them now.

So, if a piece of stone blasted into the air and on
through all the filtering limbs of the forest
to strike its rough and heavy fisted hand
like an annunciating angel against Whitney's forehead,
gesturing in that mute crushing language of rock,
so that this idiocy of his shattered mind,
once and for all, would be teased out of his head,
along with all the childish teasing we'd done,

then Whitney would just keel off his cot,
roll off like a marble falling from the sill
of this one square frame of reference,
which would become his last knowledge
of how everything with a heart of stone
moves through the world
at an absolutely inhuman speed.

Puppet Therapy

I watch a man. Hands toying his totem,
he talks to the group, his fingers
playing out his words on the table.

Everyone leans in a little closer
as he fiddles with a small, green turtle
made of rubber. He explains the sinking
turtle of his self, how he wants to shed
the dark carapace he carries.

When the day begins to lag, and
the heaviness you're born to sags
through your veins, because the clouds
have muddled the blue right out of your sky,

you just drop your soul into the deep mud
of your being. You just stop. Right there.
In the middle of the road. Become a hard lump
against the black tar of the difficult day.

He shoves the turtle head inside its shell.
This is where he dwells most of his days.

Now he takes a small enameled butterfly
from the table of assorted objects.
It is made of tin. He loves its delicate mobility,

the way it inhabits the air, un-muddied,
not dirigible, the way it doesn't hold the air
inside like a breath you can never expel.

Instead, its wings, replete with color, just twitch, then
flutter, and the whole world leaps happily after.

Somehow, he knows *it is there*:
he feels a bright fluttering in the ribcage
of his gloom that is more than just
the sluggish heart pumping to survive.

He says, *this time*, he will crack the shell;
this time, he will see the quivering inside emerge,
cleave from the hard cocoon of his heaviness,

and he will see its splendid wings spread,
and a gaudy glory will hover all red and yellow
over the green and brown smudge of his life.

Independence Day

Once, visiting Bobby in the asylum,
he told me how I could set him free: all I
had to do was sign a paper at the desk,

then I could take him over the hills and
through the woods to his friend's house.

His bloodshot eyes kept blinking fast.
They kept on tearing as he wrung his hands,

and he sniffled as if he had a cold. Still,
I took the attendant's pen and brandished it

with my name dripping off the end
just as Hancock must have done
and the others on that sultry July day—

but this was February, in Vermont,
nineteen hundred and sixty-four.

I remember how the sun set that day,
how the trees cast a jumble of shadows

over the snow and the smudge of road
all the way to the flapping vynil sides

of his refuge, the snaggletoothed Cerebus
chained by the front door, how when I left,

a slow glaze of freedom had already iced
over Bobbie's eyes, as he finally unfastened
like a heavy buckle.

                    I never tried
writing like that again—*you know*—

tying your words to the end of a stick,
then just waving it like a wand.

Working in Detox

It's not about the tearful atonements they promise
and the promises they will probably break,
nor the rock-bottom details of their lives
full of the high drama of their lows,

nor their tremorous histories of drowning alive in liquor
or the pink clouds of opiates mushrooming their brains,
nor even the happy scores they talk of having made
and may again, but how, when you raise your eyes
to this one gray-stubbled face before you,

his pallor still apparent, though he doesn't shake anymore:
the earthquake-trembling of his hands subsided at last,
you hear the anger cracking the fragile vessel of his voice,
roughening his vowels to a sandpaper pitch, all because
he doesn't yet know the promises—those blessings—

not of a second chance nor whatever number
the fingers and toes of his body have become
inadequate to tally—but of more—as you wash his feet,
dry them, then slide new socks over his gnarly, ingrown nails

so he can hobble, unembarrassed, down the long,
linoleumed hall to the day room with its TV, Scrabble,
Twelve Steps on the wall, the incomplete circle
of straight-backed chairs facing the center,
and finally, the fortified screens on the windows
as if to filter out the itch and thirst, the needle fang
of wind and weather, the predatory crouch of whim;

and as you raise your eyes to those cracked
and scab-encrusted lips, pursing—then suddenly—
spraying out their sputumous invectives—
not at you—but at the world and his wife
who put him here for his own good—*and hers,*

you hear again that stranger you once were,
tolling his rosaries of resentment, red eyes
brimming with Hell, fire and self-loathing,
until something inside him—maybe a rib—popped,
and you felt a release so biblical in its intensity
you still say amen to that simple act of surrender.

Five-Story Walk-Up

I think of it sometimes: that five-story walk-up I lived in
across from the old Knickerbocker Brewery now a park.

The leonine roar at dawn of trucks starting up to carry
their burdens of beer to the run-down bars in Jersey: places

where the stench of malt reeked up from the creaking floors
tired men shuffled over, reaching through the long ends
of their shifts for a quick quaff.

                                      What I want to tell you is how clean

I kept myself among the cockroaches; how they scurried out
the crack in the oven door each time I broiled a small steak
to eat with my tomato; how the bathtub in the kitchen reminded

you of the importance of cleanliness—how that was next to eating
in its importance; and how heaven and god could only be seen

through a skylight in the shared loo on the landing as you sat
waiting for your bowels to move and the slow Earth to follow.

Trapezing in God's Country

Now in my mid-sixties, my blond hair silvering
at the temples like little wings, I've taken up *flying*.

It happens in a farmer's field, hidden
from the road, on Sunday afternoons,

the New England summer sun frowning down
like a Puritan as we gather, coven-like, to practice.

Think of it as a post-modern meditation
on getting to heaven.

How you must study and learn the way: a trick
which arcs your ambition across the mortal divide

between fear—angst—yearning—
and the ultimate achievement of grace.

How after the long climb
up the ladder's absolute verticality,

your hand must reach out from the platform
a mere arm's length

across a void of existential proportions
to that simple bar . . .

and as you feel its weight pulling
you into the empty air,

you become aware in a totally new way
of a certain imbalance in the world:

that, unlike myth, the heart will always
weigh more than the feather.

But this bar isn't meant for such revelations,
nor the passing epiphanies of second thoughts.

It is there to move you
through a series of attitudes

your reticent body must make
arching to a pose it must hold

to carry everything your body contains: heart
—stomach—brain—into the catcher's arms.

So you climb to the vantage of the platform, high

above the tawny fodder the field still sprouts,

where a solemn attendant awaits you.

He attaches lines to a sun-colored
belt at your waist to break your fall.

You ready your stance: feet apart, toes
over the edge. Then, like a confessor,
the attendant leans in,

and cocking an ear toward your mouth,
his hands still fiddling at your waist

like bees around a flower, he asks,
so what are we trying . . . this time?

You answer, he straightens, hands you
the bar and trumpets the name

for the *really simple trick* you'll perform,
and then . . . with a *ready-y-y-y—hup!*

he calls you off the board, and you hop

snapping your legs together, toes pointed   and drop . . .

into that apparent ease of flight:

but-all-around-you-the-static-world-blurs,
and-everything-inside-changes-speed.
You-try-to-slow-your-brain-to-match
your-body-to-the-bar's-steady-swing . . .

down   and up   out   and   back . . .

then   swooping   out   again . . .

until you rise   to that point   farthest away . . .

from where you began   now   suspended

only   by your knees   your   head   arms

hands   hanging down   free from the bar . . .

back arching   into the swing . . .

and your mind   free   so   free . . .

from that everyday talk-talk of how to do this-
and-that . . . the hello-goodbye and in-between
of human exchange— the shouts from below—
the accelerating-sputter-and-clutter
of neurons in flight—all of it! . . .

has subsided . . .

into this pure emptiness			of air			this one moment . . .

this point			where all gravity			has vanished . . .

. . . though only		for the briefest		blink of time . . .

but nonetheless			not			there . . .

and where some shape		its arms reaching out

suddenly swings up . . .

to-meet-that-downward-pull-you-begin-to-feel—

and-it-grabs-your-outstretched-arms			and-you-too-grab—

and-hold—not for dear life—but for everything else.

As if in Heaven

My lover has taken my picture: I stand so my face

floats on the same plane as two bodiless heads

bobbing above a marble floor you cannot see.

                                                They orbit in tandem,

part of a mobile of the famous departed we don't recognize.

They hang from filaments invisible in ordinary light,

and except for the twinkling brass hooks, tiny haloes

in the tops of their heads and the lack of bodies,

you would think they're as real as I am.

                                                One head even looks like me:

we face the same direction though his eyes look

elsewhere.

        My lover has waited a long time for this

moment to align, balancing on her good leg, with no cane,

her camera clutched and trembling in her one good hand,

and the anticipation has left me with a smirk she catches.

Then the head resembling me, his cheeks a little fuller, his eyes a little older and filled with the memories of things I may

never see, sets his mouth firmly and continues his long turn

away—just as a heavenly body would in a real heaven.

And the other head,

                        the one I haven't described yet,

bestowed with that attracting force all heavenly bodies have,

looks away from all that is mechanical: my lover's camera,

the quick click of what we often capture, and my lover's

leg brace with its polished steel joints winking in the light;

he looks at me as if all this hanging and turning still hasn't

let him forget what it was like to walk to and fro, up and

down in the earth, feeling every inch of the body's pain.

Leaving Brahms, an Elegy

It's not the sadness of the sound,
though, God knows, there are parts

when the clarinet in Brahms' quintet
slices up and down surgically searching

for that place in my chest.
Now we come to the end of the allegro,

where the strings marry
for one—no two—unified sighs.

They resolve so gently, we almost
forget the sad clarinet.

But I know you liked Bach best of all,
and there's a certain passage

at the end of the first prelude,
when Casals slips his fingers

down the cello's neck, tightening
around the base of its throat,

and the melody rises in taut measure,
then drifts, never quite releasing,

until suddenly, Casals saws the strings
for all he's worth,

levering it back up to a crescendo,
and this time, I gasp at the power.

I play it over and over,
those last passionate steps

seesawing up to a space in the air
like a blister,

where everything is so raw
I can't move.

I want to stay there—I just
want to stay there.

Wish you were here in Sober City, Where the Sun Forever Shines on Our Shirley Temples

Of course, we're lying here in plastic lounge chairs,
the garish colors of toys,

lying here in our baggy Madras shorts
with sand between our toes

as the sea breeze ruffles
a brighter blondness into our hair.

And though our sunburnt bellies
still hang over our dull, sweaty belts,
and our shades still dim the day,

there's a sharpness to the world's
once blurry definition,
we're at last able to see,

and we can also hear
the consonants of our words

where once our vowels
washed over them

like the slurring ocean pulling back
the unworkable tongues
of our lowly tides.

Not to say that this is heaven—or even
that we've become the better angels of ourselves.

We're working on it.

Mortgages and bill collectors still abound,
but there's a green in our pockets

that grows like moss around that now steadfast stone
which hasn't rolled away in a long, long time.

Serenity?—Glad you asked.

It's a gift that stays with us
like a golden anchor on a frayed line.

Sometimes the clouds blow in and block our view,
but the sun still ripens like an orange on a tree,

and today, at least, we will sit and watch it set
instead of rise before we sleep . . .

Hiroshige: Near Komakata

Are you now, my love, near Komakata?
Cry of the cuckoo! —Takao

Just like the weather in this print, a constant
yearning clouds the sky, saturating the air,

where one migratory cuckoo hovers,
beak open to the wind, her wings oaring
her tiny body toward a new home.

Beyond the far trees, dawn brightens the horizon,
though this gloom still hovers above city, river
and bird like a secret held over you
since the day you were born.

       Yes, the spirit migrates,
moves out of desire, to its final nest, but this bird,
wherever she flies, seems to find only this empty air,

the indifferent commerce below rivering home
to the solace of rice and sake, and this one red flag
rising like a skirt in the wind every time she passes.

Constant Replay

The moment I first saw the replay
of those silver planes piercing the towers:

the sky a lucid perfection of blue,
and then the silver-bodied bird-things,
each on cue, the first banking in the air,
then on through the needle's eye,
making a dark smoldering plume
rise from the tower's crisp geometry,

and a little later, the second came,
crossing the screen as if from an offstage
place to plunge, beak first, into its own
appointed tower,

                all I could say was

Holy Shit! as everybody in the hushed bar,
where the bleak location of our lives
contained the liquefaction of our souls,
looked at me—not as if I'd blasphemed,

but as if I'd reflected on something
larger than our lives, whose consequence
they didn't yet dare to utter or couldn't,

so that even the cold wagging tongues
of their ice cubes clicking in the little bells
of their glasses went silent as well.

This was not the poet in me speaking
but a speechless heart acknowledging
the silence of a skipped beat when
the possibility of life momentarily stops,
then continues where it left off.

What do we know about the world
except what we know about ourselves?

And this can take a lifetime to discover,
trying to rewrite those tapes in our heads
that play over and over the sins
we no longer want to own.

So for years after that, I fell back
into the quiet numbness of my normal
existence, where the constantly churning
little motors of outrage were muffled
and hidden from the world's eyes and ears,

a behavior my drinking buddies
mistook for an inability to communicate
beyond the four letter expletives they
had once found as profound as I had,

but which over the years has soberly
turned into something less expletive
and more forgiving than my silence,
though I cannot say how, nor why.

I only know that the dark mendicant,
who continues to appear before me
in the middle of my tremorous nights,
extending his one good hand, wears
on his head the rags of my conscience,

and that we are both made of the same cloth.

Coffee To Go

My friend calls—not too often—but often enough—to invite me
for a ride and coffee. A time to talk and see how the same old
countryside has changed through the windshield with the season.

The apple blossoms in the orchard are his favorite,
then the roadside sugar maples blushing through a gray
autumn mist, but never the strident, white snow-devils

swirling through an open field in the late winter sun,
nor the black-boned trees of an overcast November.

He doesn't like winter. He just stays home like a bear,
though occasionally we will stir out into that season
or the early spring which is still winter.

A retired therapist, he's used to initiating talk,
but not engaging in that day-to-day-give-and-take
of recent experience, which friends usually share,

and even less so sharing those subtle misgivings
that living in a mortal and imperfect world
forces each of us to confront.

Usually, I see self-effacement as manifest humility,
but in this case, his reticence becomes a strategy
of maintaining the psychological upper hand.

Maybe I'm selling him short by not
expressing an interest in what he writes,
and so, I don't ask the right questions

which would open him like a clam to a clam lover,
showing the gray and off-white innards he holds
so dearly inside his gray and white shell.

But I do ask questions. At least, I always ask how he is,
and I'm always answered by that same belabored response
about the vein-opening weather. Or that famous singsong quote,

it's a beautiful day in the neighborhood.

We talk weather, then the incidentals of poetry. We drive
about as he maneuvers our conversation with gossip
or a question about someone we—or I—just know.

It's a countermove to what I might be thinking. He knows
I'm an easy mark to carp about my plight or others.

Now after years, he's back to asking for signed copies
of my poems each time we circle home, as if, barely able
to even walk, he'll still outlive me, and I begin to see

this is his way of grasping at the brass ring.
If he can outlast me, he will gain a certain
immortality he thinks my poems give me.

It will rub off on him. Like the ink of my signature.
I should be flattered, as I once was,

but the cost of paper being what it is
and my pension just lapping, out of reach,
at the ragged shore of my own life . . .

where I expect I will stand, toes in the sand, until I die,
staring at where the bleak sky meets the churlish ocean,
trying to discern with my failing eyes

the exact line where they join.

Chasing the Bear From the Birdfeeder

Boo! works the first time. A little less the second.
Then he begins to realize you are neither god
nor ghost, that what shines at him in the night,
your flashlight, has no power other than to reveal.
Meanwhile, the cat in the house has gone wild
with the urgency of annunciation.
                                         Outside,
something big mouses the seeds as she imagines
a rough beast slouching up to tongue out her existence.
But you, you see only a bear, the color of night,
shifting from left to right, backing away like a wrestler,
until he shuffles past the fuzzy edge of the woods
and on into the treed sanctuary you dare not enter.

Imagine a realm where all of winter is sleep.
What dreams could hold you that long?

The Woodbine's Song

> *What is the telephone pole good for*
> *if not the woodbine?*   —Ruth Stone

If you were that vine growing
where party lines used to vein
the countryside,

           and neighbor
listened to neighbor, you'd climb
toward the untouchable

human sounds humming
into the wires' sway.

           Hugging
its tarred and deadened skin, you'd

hunger for the pole's dull poetry,
the invisible fruit of its lines—

the knit-one-purl-two cup
of everyday sugar and salt—

and the ghost who calls you
through its cords of sound.

Every Poet Needs a Brother

He will be a beggar—
no, a barber!

And he will polish your nails
each time you lay down your pen

even though hair
is his only *métier*.

And he will practice the close measure
of each thin line which grows from your head,

cropping them all
to their proper lengths.

He will think you're a genius
even though he's illiterate.

For he will know, as only he can,
how the true sound of song,

which wells up in his soul,
is matched only by your words.

And you will laugh at him for years
for this simple act of faith.

But when you die, he will still shave you,
dress you in your blue serge suit,

the one you bought for this occasion
when money was of no consequence.

And he will ask alms for your burial,
because you died penniless,

now making him the beggar
you always thought he was.

Still, he will gain the pennies
necessary to cover your eyes.

And he will cross your hands over the hollow place
where once your heart was,

but now, bequeathed to someone else,
beats inside another's body

whose brother is also a barber.
And in this odd new migration of things,

where the little pieces of yourself
are finally free of each other,

you will find your heart cannot speak
to the new body it inhabits.

It cannot tell the stranger it lives in
to love his brother as you have never done.

Portrait of the Real Toad

> *nor till poets among us [. . .] can present [. . .] 'imaginary gardens with real toads in them' shall we have it.*
> ~Marianne Moore

One can go hungry in this place
where the fly's wing shines
with imagination's effervescence,
and amid the water lilies' consequential blooms
the burgeoning bugs disappear
beyond the very tip of my tongue,
their lidless eyes winking into verse.

So I have learned to put hunger
aside, to sublimate all desire—even
this unconscious tic of my tongue
shooting out this mirage of words
is a mere spasm meant to tell you
that I'm vivid while the images
around me are stiff and mythical.

Each night the garden loses color
when the poet slumbers, the pale moon
blanches out the abundant squills,
and I am allowed my one small freedom.
Only then, do I dare peep out to the scaly hearts
of my own kind, those throaty love songs
which spawn the pollywogs of my immortality.

The River Merchant's Answer to his Wife

The lights of Cho-fu-Sa fade in the distance,
and this will arrive when I do.

Travel has unraveled all my senses; each night
I curl my body around a small piece of silence
waiting in the dark for its sound.

Now, my boat rounds the point, the sky lightens,
and at last, I begin to hear the monkeys
serenade beneath our window.

I will watch for the silk flag of your sleeve
fluttering on the shore, calling me
to the slim ivory of your wrist.

I promise you we shall grow old together
feeding lychees to the monkeys
each night before we sleep.

Gran'mère Shows Us Her Crooked Finger

Beside the cemetery,
her white house radiates
(éblouissante!) in the sun
so that the gray stones
seem to grow so low

we cannot see through
the un-scythed grass
how close
death lies
to her home.

She gives us *crêpes* so big
she has to fold them & the blood red
lumps of jam *(aux fraises!)*
into wedges our little hands
can hardly hold. Beneath the eaves

paper wasps buzz out
of their own frail house
tick-less-tock-less time,
a zigzag sound. She points
à quelque chose we cannot see

above our heads, near the sky,
but what fascinates
is the long arthritic dip
between the first and second
knuckles of her finger.

Ma soeur laughs, but I can't
imagine I will *m'en souviens,*
years later, as I hold your hand
and press it to my lips.

How the Old Make Love . . .

1.

By memory. By the numbers
attached to each memory,

counting from the first time
they touched each other's
goose-bumped skin to the fourth time

they found themselves naked in a field,
the yellow splotch of sun smearing them

both with the painful stain of passion,

the tawny grass beneath their bodies
tickling and stabbing their privates.

2.

In the secrecy of memory, and the nth time
they shared just their lower halves
for an uninterrupted quickie,

their pale thighs and buttocks
gleaming in the dark

between the gloomy stacks of the library,
the oversized art books looming down

as they both looked up, gasping at the far
EXIT's red glow for a sign

their bodies would never part.

3.

Now, ever so often,
in the long gray gloaming of love

as they run their fingers
over the wrinkles of their lives,

one of them sees another face slip into place
where the other should be,

but in this long-distance dance
they've been doing together,

their lungs still full of sighs,
the heart never even skips a beat.

The Uncapping

A friend once told me this story
as I was on my way to a wedding.

It happened deep in the woods
on a ridge somewhere west of where
he lived: a woman he once loved
led him there down path after path,
reading signs only she could see,
to show him a secret place in the earth,
shown to her many years before.

It was capped with a nondescript rock
no one would have ever noticed,
which still took all her small weight
to push aside showing the entrance
to an ancient beehive chamber.

Inside: a circular stone wall rose
from the earthen floor, then arced
inward to form a dome making it
seem impossible to scale back up.

He couldn't believe they climbed in,
so that small opening—its light—
became the only link between them
and the outer world—that they stayed
waiting in the dark, as long as it took,
to see how the buried past hunched
its earth and stone shoulders over them,

and then, they made the difficult
climb out into the rest of their lives.

Notes

"Playing With Szymborska": lines in this poem allude to and/or play off lines in poems of hers as translated by Stanislaw Baranczak and Clare Cavanagh. They are as follows:

The line "The lost paradise of improbabilities" plays off lines in "Railroad Station."
The lines "We dig our toes into the clean / but gritty inches of its landscape" refer to lines in "Among Multitudes."
The third of and fourth stanzas allude to her poem, "Photograph of September 11."
The very last line of the poem alludes to S.'s poem, "Conversation With a Stone."

"After the Master, I Stay Inside": I guess I am actually referring to three masters: first, Charles Wright (hence the pun), then, Li Po and his drunken shadow in the moonlight, and, lastly, to W.B. Yeats at the end of the poem.

"Shelter": The title refers to the first Emily Dickinson epigraph at the beginning of the book and the full epigraph from "Upon Julia's Clothes" by Robert Herrick (which I felt was too cumbersome to include) is as follows:

> *Whenas in silks my Julia goes,*
> *Then, then (methinks) how sweetly flows*
> *That liquefaction of her clothes.*
>
> *Next, when I cast mine eyes, and see*
> *That brave vibration each way free,*
> *O how that glittering taketh me!*

"*La Belle Dame Sans Merci*" (the beautiful lady without mercy), of course, alludes to Keats' poem of the same title. The English equivalents to the French are: "my little fellow/man" for *mon petit bonhomme*, "in bed" for *au lit*, "isn't that so" for *ne'est-ce pas*.

"Trapezing in God's Country": in the lines "that, unlike myth, the heart will always / weigh more than the feather." I am referencing the Ancient Egyptian myth where to enter the afterlife the deceased's heart needed to weigh less than a feather.

"Hiroshige: Near Komakata": is based on woodblock number 62 in the book *One Hundred Famous Views of Edo* published by George Braziller and the Brooklyn Art Museum as well as the haiku by Takao which is quoted in the accompanying text.

"The River Merchant's Answer to his Wife," of course, plays off that famous translation of Li Po's "The River-Merchant's Wife" by Ezra Pound. The scope and depth of the Pound/Li Po poem far exceeds mine, but, alas, we keep on trying.

"*Gran'mère* Shows Us Her Crooked Finger" The code switching is meant to give to monolingual readers a sense of what bilingual speakers often do unconsciously. Quickly insertable English equivalents for non-French speakers are: "grandma" or grandmother for *gran'mère*, "dazzling" for *éblouissante*, "strawberry" *(aux fraise)* jam, "my sister" for *ma soeur* and "remember this" would replace *m'en souviens*.

About the Author

Tim Mayo lives and writes in Brattleboro, Vermont, where he is also a mental health worker at the Brattleboro Retreat and a substitute teacher. He holds an ALB, cum laude, from Harvard University and an MFA in Writing & Literature from Bennington College. He's also been studying circus arts and flying trapeze at the New England Center for Circus Arts in Brattleboro, Vermont, off and on for the last ten years.

His previous publications include a book of poetry, *The Kingdom of Possibilities* (Mayapple Press, 2009), which was a finalist for the 2009 May Swenson Award and a chapbook, *The Loneliness of Dogs* (Pudding House Publications, 2008), which was a finalist in the WCDR 2008 Chapbook Challenge in Ajax, Ontario, Canada.

Tim Mayo's work has appeared in a long list of journals, and his many awards include the International Merit Award from *Atlanta Review* 1999 and 2000; Finalist in the 2009 Paumanok Poetry Award Contest and five Pushcart nominations.

A Note on the Type

The interior typeface is Adobe Garamond Pro, designed by Robert Slimbach in 1989 as an interpretation of original roman and italic faces by the French type designers Claude Garamond (1505-1561) and Robert Granjon (1530-1590).

About Phoenicia Publishing

Phoenicia Publishing is an independent press based in Montreal but involved, through a network of online connections, with writers and artists all over the world. We are interested in words and images that illuminate culture, spirit, and the human experience. A particular focus is on writing and art about travel between cultures—whether literally, through lives of refugees, immigrants, and travelers, or more metaphorically and philosophically—with the goal of enlarging our understanding of one another through universal and particular experiences of change, displacement, disconnection, assimilation, sorrow, gratitude, longing and hope.

We are committed to the innovative use of the web and digital technology in all aspects of publishing and distribution, and to making high-quality works available that might not be viable for larger publishers. We work closely with our authors, and are pleased to be able to offer them a greater share of royalties than is normally possible.

Your support of this endeavor is greatly appreciated.

Our complete catalogue is online at www.phoeniciapublishing.com

www.ingramcontent.com/pod-product-compliance
Lightning Source LLC
LaVergne TN
LVHW041338080426
835512LV00006B/514